SCIENCE OF FUN STUFF

Looking Up!
The Science of
Stargazing

by meteorologist Joe Rao
illustrated by Mark Borgions

Ready-to-Read

Simon Spotlight
New York   London   Toronto   Sydney   New Delhi

SIMON SPOTLIGHT

An imprint of Simon & Schuster Children's Publishing Division
1230 Avenue of the Americas, New York, New York 10020
This Simon Spotlight edition April 2017
Text copyright © 2017 by Simon & Schuster, Inc.
Illustrations copyright © 2017 by Mark Borgions

For information about special discounts for bulk purchases, please contact Simon & Schuster Special Sales at
1-866-506-1949 or business@simonandschuster.com.
The Simon & Schuster Speakers Bureau can bring authors to your live event. For more information or to book an
event contact the Simon & Schuster Speakers Bureau at 1-866-248-3049 or visit our website at
www.simonspeakers.com.
Manufactured in the United States of America 0317 LAK
2 4 6 8 10 9 7 5 3 1
Cataloging-in-Publication Data for this title is available from the Library of Congress.
ISBN 978-1-4814- 7918-9 (hc)
ISBN 978-1-4814-7917-2 (pbk)
ISBN 978-1-4814-7919-6 (eBook)

CONTENTS

CHAPTER 1
The Sun and Moon

Have you ever stepped outside and looked up at the sky? Have you ever wondered about the Sun, Moon, and planets? There's a wonderful universe out there that you can't even begin to imagine. This book can help you see it.

So, let's look at the sky!

The collection of planets and their moons circling our Sun, together with smaller celestial objects in the form of asteroids, meteoroids, comets, dust, and gas make up our **solar system**. Everything in the solar system revolves around the Sun. So it makes sense for us to learn about this very important star first.

The Sun

The brightest and most important star in our sky is about ninety-three million miles away. We see the Sun as a large yellow ball only because we are much closer to the Sun than to any of the other stars.

The Sun is a tremendously hot ball of gas—the temperature of the surface of the Sun is ten thousand degrees Fahrenheit, but at its center it's twenty-seven *million* degrees Fahrenheit!

Compared to Earth, the Sun is enormous: It measures 865,000 miles across. We'd need more than a million planets the size of our Earth to fill it up!

The Sun is a gigantic nuclear furnace, generating heat through atomic energy. The intense heat and light of the Sun fuel all life on Earth.

It's sometimes possible to see dark spots, called sunspots, moving slowly across the Sun. These are giant magnetic storms on the Sun's surface, measuring from a few hundred feet to more than eighty thousand miles wide.

Occasionally there are solar flares, where a stream of particles with lots of electrical energy is shot out into space. Some of these particles become attracted to the magnetic poles of our Earth, producing electrical currents strong enough to interfere with our radio transmissions and cause static.

As those particles pass through our upper atmosphere, they can strike the gases in it, making them glow eerily with beautiful colored lights called the **aurora borealis**, or northern lights. These colored lights are seen most often near Earth's North Magnetic Pole, like northern Canada, Alaska, and Greenland. But farther south, they are seen much less frequently.

Fun Sun Fact: If you weigh one hundred pounds on Earth, you would weigh almost three thousand pounds on the Sun!

The Moon

After the Sun, the next most important object in the Earth's sky is our Moon, which shines brightly almost every night (except around the time of new moon, when it's too close to the Sun to be seen). Sometimes you can even see the Moon during the day.

Although four hundred times smaller than the Sun, the Moon is four hundred times closer to Earth, at an approximate distance of 239,000 miles away. So both the Sun and Moon appear the same size in our sky.

The Moon is the Earth's only natural satellite. A natural satellite is a space body that orbits a planet, a planetlike object, or an asteroid.

The Moon doesn't shine on its own. We see it thanks to reflected sunlight. In other words, we see the amount of the Moon lit by sunlight as it orbits around the Earth.

The Moon circles the Earth
every twenty-eight days, and as it moves
around the Earth, the angle it makes with
the Sun in our sky changes, causing the
Moon to change shape, from a crescent to a
half-moon, then a full moon, and then back
to a crescent.

Did you know? The word "month" comes
from the root word "moon" because it takes
approximately a month for the Moon to circle
the Earth.

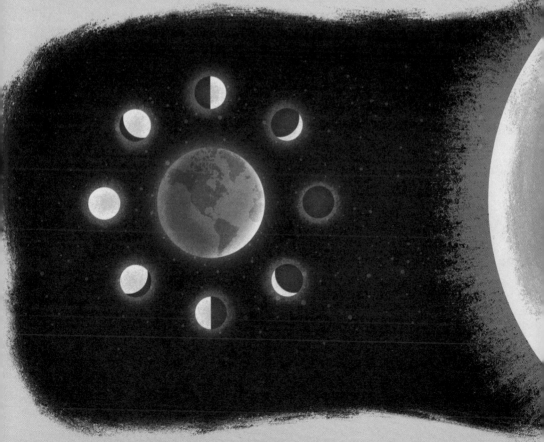

CHAPTER 2
The Stars

Our Sun is just one of countless numbers of stars. The other stars are so far away that their light, although traveling at more than eleven million miles per minute, takes many years to reach us. The light we see from the Sun left it just more than eight minutes ago. But it took the light from Sirius, the brightest of all other stars in our sky, over eight *years* to reach us!

For the more distant stars, it can take hundreds, even thousands of years for their light to reach us. And the light from other galaxies far beyond our own has taken millions of years to get here.

The total number of stars in our Milky Way galaxy has been estimated to be anywhere from one hundred billion to four hundred billion.

How many stars do you think you would be able to see on a dark, clear night? If you guessed a huge number like a million, you'd be far off the mark. In fact, no more than about 2,500 are visible at any one time. Big cities are surrounded by smoke and haze and bright lights, making it difficult to see many stars. However, people who live in small villages and towns without many streetlights are still lucky enough see a lot of stars on a clear night.

Thousands of years ago, before electricity was invented, people could see many stars on any clear night and told stories using patterns of stars to form pictures.

These patterns . . . the **constellations** . . . are the result of their imagination.

All the constellations are marked by stars whose positions haven't changed noticeably over the ages. "Fixed stars" the ancients called them, although today astronomers know that they're moving rapidly in different directions. But because they're so far away, they won't change their places in the sky for us during our entire lives.

If you've ever played the game "connect the dots," you can find constellations. But instead of dots, you'll be using stars. In the springtime, if you head outside as soon as it gets fully dark, look directly overhead for the constellation Ursa Major. Its name is Latin for "great bear."

The seven brightest stars in Ursa Major form a star pattern known as the Big Dipper, which resembles a pot with a bent handle. (See seven yellow stars in Ursa Major on page 15.)

The two outer stars in the bowl of the Big Dipper point to Polaris, the North Star.

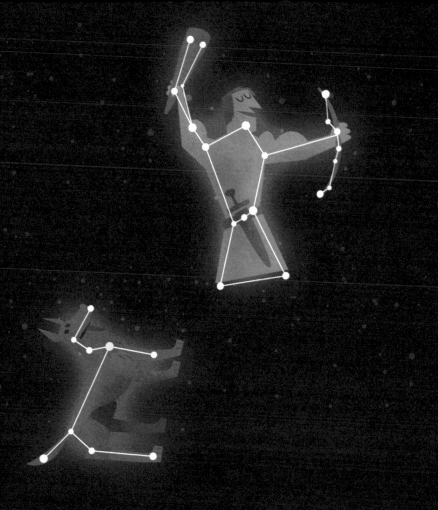

The constellation Canis Major is a dog,
who is tagging closely behind Orion,
the hunter. Canis Major includes Sirius,
the brightest star in the sky. (See yellow
star on neck.) You can see Orion in the
wintertime. Two stars mark his shoulders,
two more his knees, and three stars in a
row make up his belt.

CHAPTER 3
The Planets

But in addition to the fixed stars, there were other celestial objects known to the ancients. Although there are currently eight planets in the solar system: Mercury, Venus, Earth, Mars, Jupiter, Saturn, Uranus, and Neptune, there are only five you can see with the naked eye. (Pluto was once considered a planet, but it is now a "dwarf planet." More on Pluto later.)

To ancient people, these five bright starlike objects seemed to move almost randomly against the background of fixed

stars. The ancients called these moving stars "planets," using a Greek word meaning "wandering star."

They were different in one other way too. While the fixed stars twinkled, these five shone with a steady light. **Stars twinkle** because they appear as teeny pinpoints of light as seen from Earth, even through a telescope. **Planets don't twinkle** because they are closer, and thus appear larger in our sky, as tiny disks instead of pinpoints.

Mercury

The planet nearest to the Sun, just thirty-six million miles away, is also the smallest, scarcely bigger than our Moon. As the innermost planet, it's also the fastest moving. That's why it is named after fleet-footed Mercury, the messenger of the gods. It orbits the Sun once in only eighty-eight days. The Earth's orbit lasts for 365 days!

The Sun appears about two and a half times bigger in the daytime sky of Mercury compared to Earth, and temperatures climb to 800 degrees Fahrenheit. But at night, the temperature can drop to -280 degrees Fahrenheit.

Venus

The next planet is sixty-seven million miles away from the sun, and is by far the brightest of all the planets. For that reason the ancients named it for the goddess of beauty, Venus.

At first glance Venus looks like a lovely place to live. However, its surface is hidden by spiraling clouds of sulfuric acid within a thick atmosphere of carbon dioxide that traps the Sun's heat, causing temperatures to rise to more than 800 degrees Fahrenheit—hotter even than Mercury!

Earth

Our beautiful planet Earth is the third planet from the sun, which is about ninety-three million miles away. The Earth's **diameter** (the distance from one side to the other through Earth's center) is 7,926 miles.

Even though most of us don't need to swim to work or school, you could call Earth a water planet, as two-thirds of Earth is covered by ocean. Earth's surface rotates about its axis at 1,532 feet per second—slightly more than a thousand miles per hour—at the equator.

Did you know? Astronauts viewing the Earth from space have said it looks like a "big blue marble" because of all the oceans.

Mars

One planet stands out from all the others because of its color, appearing a distinctive orange-red hue. In ancient times this color reminded people of blood, so this planet was named for the god of war, Mars.

Mars is roughly half the size of Earth and is 142 million miles away from the Sun, taking 687 days to revolve around the Sun. It also has two very tiny moons, each not more than fourteen miles across.

For a long time people believed that dark streaks appearing to come and go on the planet's surface were canals made by intelligent beings. But our ideas about Mars changed in 1965, when *Mariner 4*, a robotic spacecraft flew past it and surprised us with views of craters and bare ground looking very similar to the Moon. As it turned out, the so-called canals were optical illusions and never existed at all! Mars is much colder than Earth and has a very thin atmosphere composed mainly of carbon dioxide. If there is, or ever was, life on Mars, we still haven't found it.

Jupiter

The next planet out from the Sun, at a distance of 484 million miles, is named after the king of the gods, and is also the king of the planets, Jupiter. It's a gigantic ball of gas and liquid almost eighty-nine thousand miles wide, made up of hydrogen and helium, and cloaked in bands of swirling, changing, multi-colored clouds of ammonia and methane. Jupiter's best known feature is the Great Red Spot, a giant hurricane-like storm that has been raging in Jupiter's thick atmosphere for more than three hundred years.

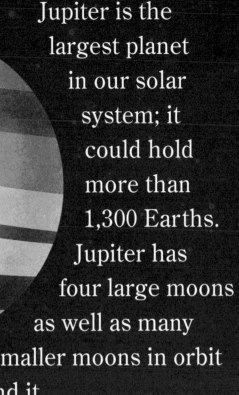

Jupiter is the largest planet in our solar system; it could hold more than 1,300 Earths. Jupiter has four large moons as well as many smaller moons in orbit around it.

When it is visible, Jupiter is often the brightest object in the sky (unless Venus, which is brighter, is also visible). Its four large moons are easily visible with binoculars; a few bands and the Great Red Spot can be seen with a small telescope.

Saturn

To the ancients, this was the slowest moving of the five planets they could see with their eyes. It would take almost thirty years to make one complete trip around the Sun. So they named it after Saturn, the god of time. Saturn is 888 million miles from the Sun, and at nearly seventy-five thousand miles across, it's the second largest planet in the solar system.

Like Jupiter, Saturn is a big ball of gas wrapped in bands of hydrogen and helium. But what makes Saturn the most beautiful planet are its remarkable rings, made up of billions of particles of ice, ranging in size from tiny specks to flying mountains measuring miles across. The rings are probably the remnants of a moon that came too close and was ripped apart by Saturn's gravity.

Saturn looks like a bright yellow star shining with a steady light, but the rings are visible only with a telescope. It has one big moon, bigger than Mercury, as well as dozens of much smaller moons.

One interesting fact about Saturn is that it's less dense than water. So, if you could find a bathtub big enough to drop Saturn into it, it would float!

Besides the six planets listed, including our own planet Earth, there are two more planets, Uranus and Neptune. You need good binoculars or a telescope to see these two planets.

Uranus

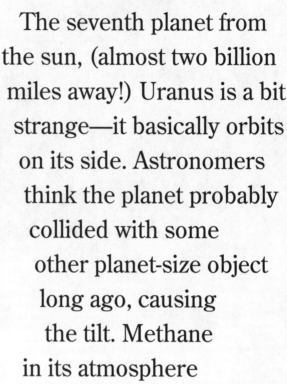

The seventh planet from the sun, (almost two billion miles away!) Uranus is a bit strange—it basically orbits on its side. Astronomers think the planet probably collided with some other planet-size object long ago, causing the tilt. Methane in its atmosphere gives Uranus its minty green tint. It has numerous moons and faint rings.

Neptune

Neptune is the eighth planet from the sun. It is almost three billion miles away!

It's known for its strong winds—sometimes faster than the speed of sound. Neptune is cold with a rocky core. The planet is more than thirty times as far from the Sun as Earth.

What About Pluto?

In 2006, the International Astronomical Union ruled to call Pluto a "dwarf planet," reducing the number of "real planets" in our solar system to eight.

However, astronomers are now hunting for another planet in our solar system, a true ninth planet, after evidence of its existence was unveiled on January 20, 2016. So we may be learning about a brand-new ninth planet very soon!

THE PLANETS:
- Mercury
- Venus
- Earth
- Mars
- Jupiter
- Saturn
- Uranus
- Neptune
- Pluto

CHAPTER 4
Meteors and Comets

Occasionally the ancients would notice something that made them think that a star had fallen from the sky. We call them **meteors** today, although the terms "falling star" and "shooting star" are widely used.

Today we know that meteors are caused by tiny flecks of dust particles or debris crashing into our atmosphere, usually disappearing in a bright streak or flash. Larger chunks sometimes survive and are found on the ground. If so, they become geologic specimens called **meteorites**.

At certain times of year the Earth runs into a stream of comet dust, and you can see a "shower" of meteors in the sky.

Best nights of the year to see meteors: August 11, 12, 13 and December 12, 13, 14. Look overhead and toward the northeast after ten p.m.

Other mysterious moving objects in the sky are **comets**. Professional astronomers can count on observing about half a dozen at almost any time, but comets bright enough to excite those of us without big telescopes are rare, as few as one or two every ten to twenty years. Today we know comets are made of frozen gases that are heated as they approach the Sun and made to glow by the Sun's light. As the gases warm and expand, the solar wind blows the expanding material out into the comet's beautiful tail. To ancient observers the head resembled a head of long hair, so they called comets "hairy stars."

CHAPTER 5
Eclipses of the Moon and Sun

An eclipse of the Moon takes place when the Sun, Earth, and Moon are aligned in such a way that the Earth throws its shadow onto the full moon and blocks off sunlight from reaching the Moon. If the Moon is completely within the Earth's shadow, we say there is a total eclipse. If only a part of the Moon is in the shadow, we call that a partial eclipse.

Interestingly, during a total eclipse the Moon usually doesn't disappear. Instead, it tends to glow a coppery red color because as sunlight passes the Earth, our atmosphere acts like a lens and bends the red colors we see at sunrise and sunset into the Earth's shadow and onto the Moon. In some years there may be no eclipses of the Moon, or as many as two or three. An eclipse of the Moon can be seen wherever the Moon is above the horizon when the eclipse is taking place, that is to say, over half of the world.

Future total eclipses of the Moon
for North America:
January 20, 2019
May 15, 2022
November 8, 2022
March 13, 2025

Eclipses of the Sun

An eclipse of the Sun takes place when the Moon, in its orbit around the Earth, moves between the Earth and the Sun and blocks off the view of the Sun from part of the Earth. If the Moon covers the entire Sun, we say there is a total eclipse. If only a part of the Sun is hidden by the Moon, we call that a partial eclipse.

Most of the time eclipses of the Sun take place over areas where few people live, like the Pacific Ocean or the North Pole. And most eclipses of the Sun are partial. A total eclipse can be seen only when the Moon's dark shadow cone, called the umbra, touches the Earth.

CHAPTER 6
Mark Your Calendars!

Be sure to place a big red circle around Monday, August 21, 2017.

On that special day, for the first time since 1918 the dark shadow cone of the Moon will sweep from coast to coast across the United States along a sixty-eight-mile-wide track which astronomers call the "path of totality."

Since the Moon's shadow moves very rapidly, the Sun will not be completely hidden for very long . . . no more than two minutes and forty seconds. Across all of North America, as well as Alaska and Hawaii, the Moon will appear to cover at least a part of the Sun. Just how much of the Sun will be hidden by the Moon depends on where you live.

If you live very close to the path of totality, you'll see only a sliver of the Sun remaining. If that's the case, most definitely you should try to make an effort to get inside the totality path because only

Seattle 92%
10:20 A.M.

Helena 92%
11:34 A.M.

100% TOTALITY	
Salem, OR 10:17 A.M.	Casper, WY 11:42 A.M.
Columbia, MO 1:12 P.M.	Nashville, TN 1:27 P.M.
Charleston, SC 2:46 P.M.	

San Francisco 76%
10:15 A.M.

Denver 92%
11:47 A.M.

Los Angeles 62%
10:21 A.M.

Austin 65%
1:10 P.M.

Tucson 59%
10:36 A.M.

when the Sun is completely covered will you see a **total eclipse**! If, on the other hand, you live far away from the path of totality, like Hawaii, it will appear like only a small "bite" has been taken out of the Sun.

Check out the map to see what you'll see from your home.

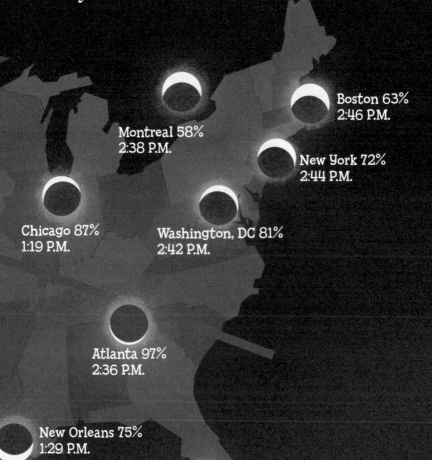

Montreal 58%
2:38 P.M.

Boston 63%
2:46 P.M.

New York 72%
2:44 P.M.

Chicago 87%
1:19 P.M.

Washington, DC 81%
2:42 P.M.

Atlanta 97%
2:36 P.M.

New Orleans 75%
1:29 P.M.

Miami 78%
2:58 P.M.

What Happens During a
Total Eclipse of the Sun?

Here's what you'll see if you're lucky to
be inside the totality path: The day starts
off bright and sunny.

A while later it almost seems like a
thunderstorm is brewing. Then suddenly,
the midsummer day will turn strangely
dark.

A few stars come out. Birds and animals
become confused and quickly head home
to sleep! Night insects begin to chirp!

Meanwhile, up in the sky where the Sun
should be, there appears instead a

jet-black disk surrounded by a softly glowing white halo, called the **corona.**

And as the corona first forms, there might be a brief flash of light, as the last rays of sunlight sweep behind the rugged rough edge of the Moon, creating a huge diamond ring in the sky!

Then, just a couple of precious minutes later, it's over. The sky brightens up. The stars disappear, birds and animals awaken, and the sun returns. It is all very strange and eerie, and it is no wonder that long ago people thought the world was nearing its end.

Ancient Eclipses

People in the distant past were keenly aware that if the Sun were to suddenly disappear, all life on Earth would end. For this reason, before science had an explanation for this event, people often feared solar eclipses. Because the sunlight seemed to get weaker as the eclipse

progressed, some may have thought that the Sun was sick or that evil spirits were attacking the Sun. During an eclipse, people would beat drums, dance wildly, and make as much noise as possible in order to chase the spirits away.

Different cultures were confused by eclipses and tried to explain them as a time when demons or animals devoured the Sun. The Chinese, for instance, thought that a dragon was eating the

Sun and tried scaring it away by beating drums and shooting arrows into the sky. On October 22, 2137 BCE, two Chinese astronomers whose job it was to carefully watch the sky failed to alert people that an eclipse was taking place on that day. As a result, the people were caught completely off guard. During the eclipse, there was widespread panic everywhere. The emperor was furious and the guards were punished. Eventually, after many centuries, astronomers in the Middle East who had kept records of past eclipses were able to use them to predict future eclipses.

And have you ever heard of someone being "scared to death?" That actually happened in the year 840, when the timid Emperor Louis of Bavaria witnessed a total solar eclipse, and immediately after it finished, he died of fright!

But don't *you* be scared, because there is no reason to be!

Do NOT use to view a solar eclipse.

However . . .

Eclipses *can* be dangerous. Countless numbers of people over the ages have had their eyes severely burned from looking too long at the darkening Sun because the sunlight can permanently injure your eyes and cause blindness.

Did we frighten you with that warning?

Well, we didn't really mean to, but we did mean to stress that there are many *wrong ways* to look at a solar eclipse, and that using one of these wrong ways can lead to eye damage.

People often think that they can watch an eclipse by using smoked glass, X-ray films, sunglasses, and camera filters. This is a big mistake. Although the Sun may appear much dimmer when looking through these filters, the Sun's invisible infrared rays are still passing through.

Since there are no nerves in the retina of your eyes, no pain is felt while the damage is occurring. So your eyes can be burned without you even being aware of it! It's also dangerous to look directly at the Sun through binoculars or a telescope.

But it's perfectly safe to look at a solar eclipse using one of the correct ways. . . .

One way is to make a pinhole in a piece of thin cardboard. Hold the cardboard so the image of the Sun can pass through the pinhole onto a sheet of white paper. This pinhole projection of the image of the eclipsed Sun is the safest of all viewing techniques. The farther the pinhole is from the paper, the larger the image of the eclipsed Sun will be on the white paper.

Another way is to spread a bedsheet under a tree and let the Sun's light pass through the leaves. On the sheet you will see hundreds of images of the eclipse projected in the same manner as the cardboard method.

So is there is ever a time when you can watch a solar eclipse without any special precautions?

The surprising answer is yes!

For the **precious few minutes** during a total eclipse **when the entire disk of the Sun is completely covered by the Moon,** it's safe to look directly at it with your eyes and through binoculars or telescopes!

When the sun is **completely eclipsed,** feel free to look at it, take photos, and be amazed by one of Mother Nature's most spectacular sights! But as soon as the shadow begins to move and the Sun comes back out, look away or use one of the proper viewing techniques.

Being an expert on something means you can get an awesome score on a quiz on that subject! Take this

SCIENCE OF STARGAZING QUIZ

to see how much you've learned.

1. "Planet" is a Greek word which means
   - a. starry sky
   - b. wandering star
   - c. night object

2. Why can Earth be called a water planet?
   - a. It rains a lot on Earth.
   - b. No other planet has water.
   - c. Two-thirds of the Earth is covered by oceans.

3. What is the brightest star in the sky?
   - a. Sun
   - b. North Star
   - c. Moon

4. An eclipse of the Sun occurs when
   - a. the Moon moves between the Earth and the Sun, blocking the view of the Sun from Earth
   - b. the Earth blocks sunlight from reaching the Moon
   - c. the Sun is hidden by storm clouds

5. The glowing white halo formed around the Sun during a total eclipse is called
   - a. diamond ring
   - b. corona
   - c. angel effect

6. A meteor is also occasionally called a
   - a. comet
   - b. hairy star
   - c. shooting star

7. The Moon
   - a. orbits the Earth
   - b. orbits the Sun
   - c. never moves

8. During a total eclipse of the Sun
   - a. the sky darkens
   - b. a few stars appear
   - c. both a and b are correct

Answers: 1. b 2. c 3. a 4. a 5. b 6. c 7. a 8. c

48